For the Scooby Gang: Bry, Vix and Ims, and all our little scrappy doos. – S.H.

To Jacob, the GOAT! – J.B.

First published in Great Britain 2025 by Red Shed, part of Farshore
An imprint of HarperCollins*Publishers*
1 London Bridge Street,
London SE1 9GF
www.farshore.co.uk

HarperCollins*Publishers*
Macken House, 39/40 Mayor Street Upper
Dublin 1, D01 C9W8, Ireland

Red Shed is a registered trademark of HarperCollins*Publishers* Ltd.

Text copyright © Swapna Haddow 2025
Illustrations copyright © Jess Bradley 2025
Swapna Haddow and Jess Bradley have asserted their moral rights.
Consultancy by Naomi Hiscock at Primary STEM Education Consultancy
and Jules Pottle.
ISBN 978 0 00 871335 5
Printed in Malaysia.
001

A CIP catalogue record for this title is available from the British Library.

All rights reserved. No part of this publication may be reproduced, stored in a retrieval system, or transmitted, in any form or by any means, electronic, mechanical, photocopying, recording or otherwise, without the prior permission of the publisher and copyright owner.

Without limiting the author's and publisher's exclusive rights, any unauthorised use of this publication to train generative artificial intelligence (AI) technologies is expressly prohibited. HarperCollins also exercise their rights under Article 4(3) of the Digital Single Market Directive 2019/790 and expressly reserve this publication from the text and data mining exception.

Stay safe online. Any website addresses listed in this book are correct at the time of going to print. However, Farshore is not responsible for content hosted by third parties. Please be aware that online content can be subject to change and websites can contain content that is unsuitable for children. We advise that all children are supervised when using the internet.

Experiments and activities are performed at your own risk, follow the instructions and ALWAYS ask an adult for help. HarperCollins is not responsible for the results of your experiments. Always ask an adult for help with any craft activity or DIY project. Wear protective clothes and cover surfaces to avoid damage or staining.

This book contains FSC™ certified paper and other controlled sources to ensure responsible forest management.

For more information visit: www.harpercollins.co.uk/green

HOW TO SAVE YOUR GRANNY FROM A RUNAWAY TRAIN

SWAPNA HADDOW & JESS BRADLEY

INTRODUCTION

The bonkers world of science has some of the answers to how things work and why things don't. In this book, you will find ridiculous and not-so-ridiculous dilemmas, which all have solutions from the magical, astonishing and unbelievable world of science. All the hard work has been done for you - thanks to brilliant scientists - but you can test out the science for yourself with an experiment at the end of each section.

Learning science at home is what Laura Bassi (1711-1778) did - and she became the first female professor of physics at a European university in 1776. (Girls weren't allowed to study science in school back then!)

You'll come away with all the knowledge you need to survive everything - including a grumpy emu and an alien invasion!

Pssst!

The brilliant thing about science is that even if it doesn't go the way you expect, you've still learned something. You've learned that it doesn't work. The magic of learning through science is that it is all about experimenting and discovering. **JUST MAKE SURE THAT YOU'VE CHECKED WITH A PARENT OR GUARDIAN BEFORE YOU START!** (They can also help with any tricky bits AND you can wow them with your new knowledge!)

CONTENTS

HOW TO . . .	
GET A FART MACHINE OUT OF YOUR CLASSROOM	8
LIFT A JUMBO JET	12
RESCUE GRANDAD FROM A VOLCANO	16
ESCAPE A DESERTED ISLAND	20
MAKE SURE GRANNY SURVIVES THE PIRATES' SLIDE	24
AVOID A GRUMPY EMU IN A MAZE	28
GET A PARTY STARTED	32
MAKE A PHONE CALL WITHOUT A PHONE	36
SPY ON SOMEONE	40
TRICK A SHARK	44
ESCAPE A GORILLA	48
SCARE OFF AN ALIEN INVASION	52
SAVE YOUR GRANNY FROM A RUNAWAY TRAIN	56
GLOSSARY	60
INDEX	61

CALAMITY COMICS

HOW TO GET A FART MACHINE OUT OF YOUR CLASSROOM

1

THE SCIENCE COMIC YOU NEVER KNEW YOU NEEDED — PHYSICS EDITION

Oh no! Archie's grandad thought it would be funny to hide a fart machine in Archie's school bag because he knows how much his teacher hates farts. But now Archie has discovered it...

Prrrpt! Guff! Brrrt!

Grandad jammed the switch...

Hee hee hee!

Guff!

...so the fart machine won't turn off!

Poot!
STOMP!
Prrrpt!

Archie needs to get it out of the second-floor classroom before the teacher arrives!

Braaap!
Pfft!
Prrrpt!

Jiggle Jiggle!

What do YOU think Archie should do ...

A) PANIC?

B) MAKE A PARACHUTE FOR THE FART MACHINE?

C) PRETEND IT'S HIS FRIEND FARTING?

Turn the book upside down to see the answers!

If you chose A, then Archie is off to see the headteacher.

If you chose B, WELL DONE - Archie's able to launch it out of the window and his teacher has no idea.

If you chose C, Archie's friend is sent to the medical room to see what's causing the farting, and so won't be there for sports day when Archie needs him to be part of the relay race.

WHAT'S THE SCIENCE?

This is all about the forces of **gravity** and **air resistance**.

Now, the reason we aren't floating away into space is because the force of gravity is keeping us on the floor. You can't see it, but it's at work all the time. That's why when you jump, you return to the ground.

But when we drop something from a height, there is also another force at work called air resistance. Air pushes back against the falling object and the larger the area of the object, the more the air slows its fall. That's how a parachute works.

Ready to put the science into action?

HAVE A GO WITH A PARACHUTE EGG DROP EXPERIMENT

Don't worry if you don't have a fart machine – have a go with eggs to help you understand gravity and air resistance. Can you get an egg to the ground without it breaking?

You will need:

- Four large bin bags
- A small plastic bag
- String
- Sticky tape
- Scissors*
- Eggs*

*Be careful – ask an adult for help with scissors and launching the eggs.

If you don't want to waste eggs because you fancy omelette for dinner, use a small piece of dough.

Instructions:

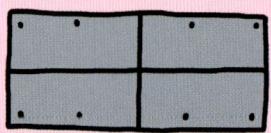

1. Cut up and stick together the bin bags to make one flat piece. Make small holes with the scissors to match the image above.

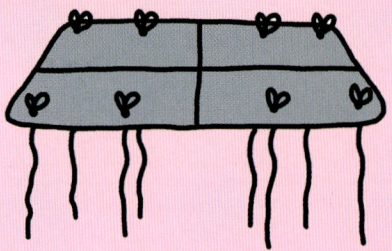

2. Thread a piece of string through one hole and secure the end with a knot. Repeat for each hole, so you have eight strings.

3. Place an egg into the small bag and secure the top. (Use sticky tape if needed.)

4. Attach the ends of each string to the top of the egg bag.

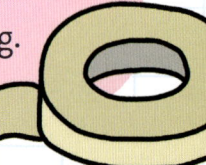

5. With an adult, take the egg with the parachute and an egg without a parachute to a window high up, where the eggs can be launched safely. Make sure the area below is clear from people, animals and objects. Drop them at the same time!

Which one was quicker? Did one land without breaking?

Try making different-sized parachutes and see how they affect the eggs' fall.

Archie doesn't want the fart machine splattered all over the playground! But, if he creates a parachute with six bin bags and throws it upwards to help the parachute inflate, this should allow it to land without too much of a bump!

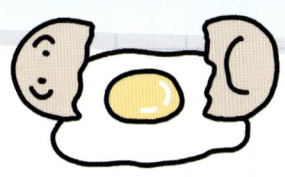

CALAMITY COMICS

HOW TO LIFT A JUMBO JET

THE SCIENCE COMIC YOU NEVER KNEW YOU NEEDED — PHYSICS EDITION

Amy's granny turned up early at the airport and was bored. So, she took the jumbo jet that was supposed to fly her family on holiday for a spin. She accidentally parked it in the field, just off the runway and now it's stuck in the grass . . .

Amy's mum and dad were at samba class last night . . .

Her dad hurt his back . . .

. . . and her mum stubbed her toe, so they can't help.

And her granny has scarpered.

It's up to Amy to work out what to do next!

Should Amy ...

A) GET THE FAMILY WALKING?

B) FORGET THE HOLIDAY AND GO HOME?

C) SHIFT THE PLANE USING A PLANK OF WOOD?

If you chose A, it would take Amy 673 days to get there if the family walked 10km per day. That's nearly two years!
If you chose B, everyone would be miserable.
If you chose C, HURRAY - everyone is heading off on holiday.

WHAT'S THE SCIENCE?

Lifting something heavy seems impossible without a giant machine, but it is entirely possible by creating a **lever**.

A lever works like a seesaw in a playground. A seesaw has a long beam that sits over a point known as a **fulcrum**. It moves up and down depending on which end you sit on. The **effort** is the force put into lifting the other side of the seesaw when you sit on one end. This is exactly the clever science needed to shift the plane - ready to test this out yourself?

Effort

Fulcrum

MAKE YOUR OWN LEVER

No plane to practise with? No worries! How about trying this out with a heavy book? Impress your friends and family by showing them how to shift the book by using one finger . . .

You will need:

- A heavy book
- A long, sturdy wooden ruler or stick
- A pen

Try different objects and see if this changes the experiment.

Instructions:

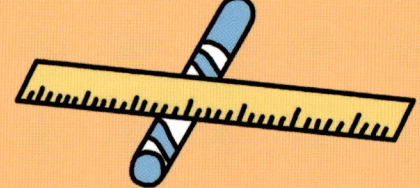

1. Lay the pen (your fulcrum) on a table and place the ruler on top.

2. Place the book on one end of the ruler.

14

3. Press the other end of the ruler and see if the book lifts off the table.

4. Move the pen closer to the book. What happens when you press the other side?

5. Now move the pen closer to your finger, and then press down on the lever. What do you notice about how much effort is needed?

Pssst! Moving the pen closer to the book will make it easier to lift.

If Amy uses a plank of wood as a beam, a barrel as a fulcrum, and makes sure the distance between where she sits on the beam and the fulcrum is longer than the distance from the plane to the fulcrum, Amy could move the plane without breaking a sweat. Okay, okay, so the plank would need to be at least 22km long and Amy would need to be about 20,000 times further away from the fulcrum compared to the jet, but in theory it is possible!

END OF PLANK 22KM AWAY

CALAMITY COMICS

3

HOW TO RESCUE GRANDAD FROM A VOLCANO

THE SCIENCE COMIC YOU NEVER KNEW YOU NEEDED — PHYSICS EDITION

It's time for a family walk. Archie's grandad reckons there is a good viewpoint at the top of the steep hill, so everyone clambers up. When they get to the top, they realise it's the crater of a dormant volcano. Just as they peer in, disaster strikes!

Archie's grandad slips and tumbles straight into the deep, dark hole . . .

Grandad isn't happy. It turns out he doesn't like being in deep holes . . .

And he can't seem to be able to climb out because he's hurt his foot.

Archie looks around for a way to get his grandad out.

Should Archie ...

A) USE SOME VINES?

B) JUMP DOWN AND KEEP GRANDAD COMPANY?

C) FIND A FALLEN TREE TO MAKE A LADDER?

If you chose **A**, YOU CHOSE RIGHT! These are perfect for creating a mechanism to pull up Grandad.

If you chose **B**, Grandad and Archie could be down there a long time.

If you chose **C**, this could have been a good idea, but it would take Archie months and months.

WHAT'S THE SCIENCE?

The solution is all about **pulleys**. A single pulley is a simple mechanism that changes the direction of the force required to lift an object. Instead of pulling the object up, which is hard, a single pulley allows you to lift the object by pulling down, which is easier. Using two or more pulleys reduces the force needed to lift the object, but a longer length of rope would be needed.

The ancient Egyptians used this scientific principle over 4,000 years ago to help them move huge, heavy stones needed for building the pyramids. And we still use pulley mechanisms today, for example in lifts, in wells to pull up buckets and in weight-lifting machines.

Pulley

MAKE YOUR OWN 'PULLEY' SYSTEM

Have a go at making your own 'pulley' to practise with, in case you ever lose someone down a volcano.

You will need:

- A long piece of ribbon or string (about 2.5-3m long)
- A one-pint plastic milk bottle filled with water
- A staircase railing*

*Be careful – ask an adult for help.

HELP SAVE GRANDAD

Need someone with strong arms. Will reward you with lots of shiny stickers.

Instructions:

1. Tie the ribbon around the handle of the milk bottle.

2. Try lifting the milk bottle with the ribbon. Is it tricky?

3. Ask an adult to loop the untied end of the ribbon around the staircase railing.

4. Try pulling down on the ribbon. It should now be easier, as you are pulling down, not lifting up.

To make this even easier, try using two 'pulleys'. To try this, ask an adult to tie one end of the ribbon to the railing, then pass the other end through the bottle handle and then over another railing.

No staircase railing? You could use a doorknob or a broom handle laid over a gap between two tables.

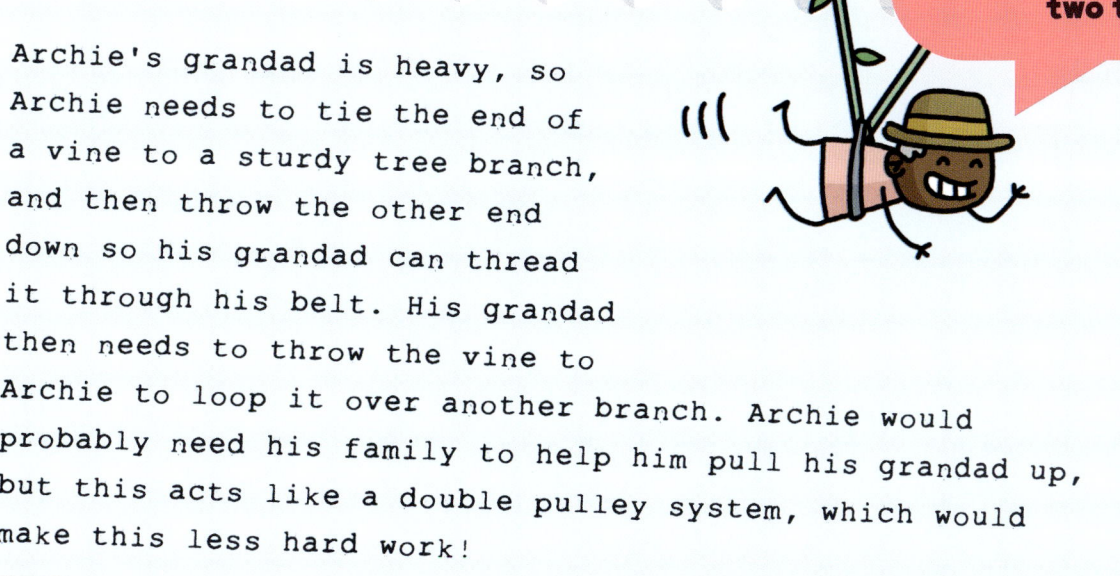

Archie's grandad is heavy, so Archie needs to tie the end of a vine to a sturdy tree branch, and then throw the other end down so his grandad can thread it through his belt. His grandad then needs to throw the vine to Archie to loop it over another branch. Archie would probably need his family to help him pull his grandad up, but this acts like a double pulley system, which would make this less hard work!

19

CALAMITY COMICS

HOW TO ESCAPE A DESERTED ISLAND

4

| THE SCIENCE COMIC YOU NEVER KNEW YOU NEEDED | PHYSICS EDITION |

Uh-oh. Mo is on a school trip on a remote island and there's a storm coming. Everyone needs to head home quickly, but no one remembers the way back – Mo is sure they've passed the tree that looks like Bigfoot three times already. There is a map, but it doesn't make sense because no one knows which way is north . . .

Rocky is convinced they should turn right and right again.

But Anika is fed up with Rocky's directions and says they should all go left.

Wei and Zoe are siding with Anika.

But Flynn and Ava want to go with Rocky.

Mo gets the deciding vote. Will they make it home in time for dinner?

Should Mo ...

A) SIT DOWN AND HOPE THEY GET RESCUED?

B) CHOOSE A DIFFERENT DIRECTION AND GO ALONE?

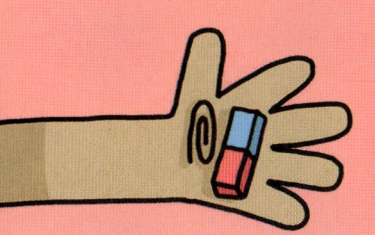

C) USE THE PAPERCLIP AND MAGNET IN HIS POCKET?

If you chose A, everyone may eventually get rescued, but it could be days before they are found.

If you chose B, sadly Mo is still wandering around the island and is about to come face to face with a wildcat.

If you chose C, YES - Mo can make a compass to find the way back.

WHAT'S THE SCIENCE?

Magnets are going to help us here. A magnet is a rock or metal that **attracts** - pulls together - certain metals (for example, iron and nickel) and rocks (for example, lodestone) towards it. One magnet can also **repel** (push apart) another magnet. If you have used toy trains with magnets or magnets at school, you may have noticed how they attract and repel.

And guess what? You are standing on the world's biggest magnet! That's right, Earth is a whopper-sized one.

Want to check out the science of magnets? Turn the page and let's give it a go!

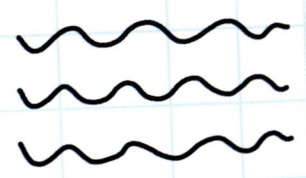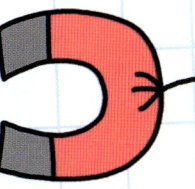

MAKE YOUR OWN COMPASS

Using a magnet and a paperclip, it's possible to make your own **compass**. It works because if you magnetise the metal of the paperclip, it lines up with Earth's magnetic field, pointing to the North Pole.*

*Confusingly, Earth's geographic North Pole is the magnetic South Pole, but using a compass to find north and following a map, can help you find your way.

You will need:
- A straightened paperclip**
- A bowl of cold water
- A small piece of card
- A magnet**

**Be careful – ask an adult for help.

One of the earliest forms of magnetic compass was used in ancient China – initially for fortune telling, rather than navigation!

Instructions:

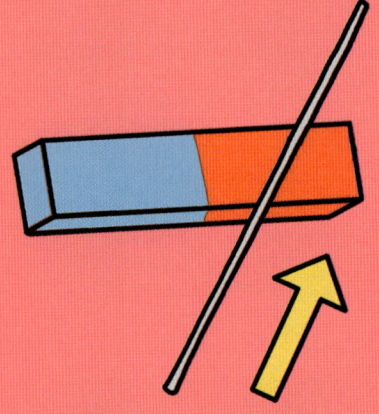

1. Rub the paperclip against one end of the magnet (in one direction only) around 100 times to magnetise it.***

2. Place the piece of card gently on the water in the bowl.

***To test if the paperclip is now magnetic, you could see if it picks up other paperclips. Try both ends.

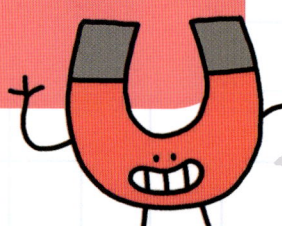

22

3. Place the magnetised paperclip on top of the card.

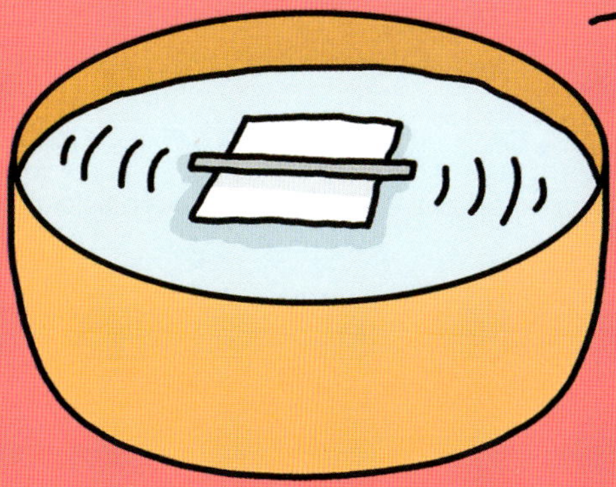

4. The paperclip will turn and should stop to line up in a north/south direction.

Compare your homemade compass with a real compass if you have one.

So, Mo needs a thin piece of metal. Luckily, he doesn't need to use the wire from Ava's braces, because he has a paperclip and a fridge magnet in his pocket. He can then set up his compass, just like you did in the experiment, using a small leaf as his card and a puddle as his bowl of water.

CALAMITY COMICS

HOW TO MAKE SURE GRANNY SURVIVES THE PIRATES' SLIDE

5

THE SCIENCE COMIC YOU NEVER KNEW YOU NEEDED — PHYSICS EDITION

Amy took her eyes off her granny for one second, **ONE SECOND**, and she's found herself in a boatload of trouble. Classic Granny has only gone and been captured by . . .

. . . Dastardly Captain Rottenleg and his scurvy pirate crew!

GULP!

So Amy's family jump aboard a boat on a rescue mission.

Oh no! Amy can see . . .

. . . that the pirates want Granny to go down their slide!

The family need more time to get to the ship – so Granny needs a plan!

Can you help? Should Granny ...

A) ASK ROTTENLEG TO ROLL OUT A RED CARPET?

B) PERSUADE ROTTENLEG TO LET HER GO?

C) CHALLENGE ROTTENLEG TO A SWORD FIGHT?

If you chose A, believe it or not, this is a BRILLIANT IDEA as it will slow Granny down.

If you chose B, this is a nice idea, but unlikely to work.

If you chose C, this is a very bad idea because Granny has a balloon sword!

WHAT'S THE SCIENCE?

Have you ever slipped on ice or a wooden floor? This is because smooth surfaces have very little **friction** (the force that works against a moving object). Friction slows down an object. The rougher the surface, the more friction created.

A long time ago, a scientist named Isaac Newton (1643-1727) noticed that friction will always try to stop or slow something that is moving. Luckily, HE didn't stop or slow down in his discoveries. We owe lots of our understanding about science to his brilliant brain.

Let's all be brilliant like Isaac Newton for a bit and have a look at friction with an experiment.

MAKE A FRICTION RAMP

Get ready to test out the friction of different materials. Which ones will let things go whizzing down? Which ones will be slow and steady? You're about to find out . . .

You will need:

- A large, smooth hardback book or a piece of wood
- A small towel
- A plastic bottle top
- A small stack of books

Instructions:

1. Place the small stack of books under one side of the large hardback book.

2. Hold the bottle top flat side down at the top of your book ramp.

3. Let go and watch the bottle top slide down.

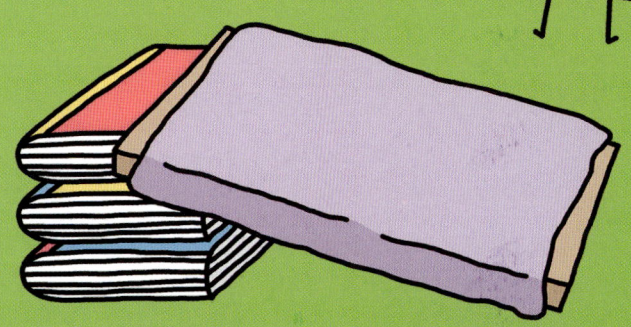

4. Now place the towel over the ramp. Make sure it is flat and covering the large book's surface.

5. Let the bottle top slide down. It should be slower!

Repeat with other materials like bubble wrap, sandpaper or a fluffy blanket. Predict which surface will be fastest and see if your predictions are right.

If Amy's granny slid down carpet, it would be slower than sliding down wood because more friction is working against her body. This would give Amy just enough time to rescue her granny as she drops off the end and into the boat. How slowly her granny goes depends on what she is wearing and how thick the carpet is. Silky clothes and a short pile carpet might be the quickest, and corduroy clothes and super-thick carpet might be the slowest!

CALAMITY COMICS

HOW TO AVOID A GRUMPY EMU IN A MAZE

6

THE SCIENCE COMIC YOU NEVER KNEW YOU NEEDED — **PHYSICS EDITION**

Amy's family are on a day out. Her dad thought it would be fun to have a wander through a hedge maze. And everyone agreed this would be fun. Her granny thought it would be fun to bring a grumpy emu to chase them around the maze. Absolutely nobody agreed this would be fun . . .

Amy is sure the exit is somewhere around here . . .

But her dad is panicking and her mum is busy telling him not to panic.

I'M PANICKING!

STOP PANICKING!

All the hedge walls are starting to look the same . . .

And Amy is sure she can hear the angry grunt of her granny's emu nearby . . .

GRUNT!

How are they going to get out of the maze safely without being pecked?

Should they ...

A) PANIC?

B) STAY STILL?

C) USE THEIR EARS?

If you chose A, nope, bad idea. Amy's mum and dad are about to become a very pecked mum and dad!

If you chose B, this could work, but staying still means the emu is likely to find them eventually.

If you chose C, WELL DONE - this will help them get out of the maze safely.

WHAT'S THE SCIENCE?

Sounds travel by vibrations. For example, when you beat a drum, the skin of the drum vibrates, and this then makes the air around the object vibrate. These vibrations travel to our ears and that's how most people can hear sounds.

Vibrations can travel through air and water, and through solid materials like bricks and glass.

It's possible to detect where a sound is coming from. When **sound waves** reach the inner ear, they are turned into electrical signals and these are sent to your brain. Parts of the brain then compare the signals from each ear to work out the direction of the sounds.

Ready to put the science of sound to the test?

SEE SOUND

It's possible to hear sound, but have you ever SEEN sound? Try out this brilliant way of seeing sound waves in action.

You will need:

- A large bowl
- Plastic wrap
- A teaspoon of uncooked rice

Instructions:

1. Put the plastic wrap over the top of the bowl and pull it tight.

2. Now put the rice on top, making sure to spread it out.

3. Sing or shout close to the bowl. Sound waves will travel from your vibrating vocal cords and make the whole bowl vibrate. This will vibrate the air inside the bowl and the plastic wrap on top. And this will make the rice move!

EXPERIMENT WITH LOCATING SOUNDS

Now see how sound changes with distance and location. It's also handy to see how far away you need to be to avoid hearing someone yelling at you to do your homework!

You will need:
- A blindfold
- A room
- At least three other people

Take turns with the blindfold so you can all have a go. Try standing closer and further away from one another. How does this affect the sounds?

Instructions:

1. Blindfold one person and stand them in the centre of a room. Then ask the other two to stand in different corners.

2. Test the blindfolded person's ability to locate sounds as the others take turns to clap.

3. Every time the blindfolded person hears a sound, they should turn in that direction. How do they get on?

If Amy and her family head in one direction, they can use their ears to listen to the emu's grunting. If the squawking gets louder, they need to go the other way to avoid being pecked!

CALAMITY COMICS

HOW TO GET A PARTY STARTED

7

| THE SCIENCE COMIC YOU NEVER KNEW YOU NEEDED | PHYSICS EDITION |

It's Wei's birthday and he can't wait to celebrate. He wants disco lights, a karaoke machine, a bouncy castle, a Ferris wheel, 44 arcade machines and a DJ of course! But the DJ got lost on the way over and Wei's uncle has used every single plug socket, so there is nowhere to plug a speaker into . . .

If Wei finds out there is no music, he will have a full-scale meltdown!

WHAT'S A PARTY WITHOUT MUSIC?

All Wei's sister has is their dad's phone and his Party Mix playlist.

But the guests can barely hear the music from the tiny speaker.

Should Wei's sister ...

A) RUN?

B) START SINGING TO ENTERTAIN EVERYONE?

C) GO TO THE TOILET AND GRAB SOME TOILET ROLLS?

If you chose A, this would save Wei's sister from the tears, foot stamping and general mayhem, but the party will still be a let-down.
If you chose B, this would buy Wei's sister some time, but a colossal Wei tantrum is still likely.
If you chose C, EXCELLENT CHOICE. Toilet-roll tubes will save the day.

WHAT'S THE SCIENCE?

All sounds travel to our ears as vibrations. Normally, the vibrations spread out and get weaker as they move further away from the source of the sound. That's why it is harder to hear someone talking at the other end of a large room.

Have you ever spoken into a megaphone? Or created a cone with a piece of card and spoken into it? Well, the sound vibrates the air both inside and outside the megaphone, which helps create a louder sound. The sound is also louder because the megaphone, or tube, **amplifies** your voice. This means it gathers the vibrations together, sending them in one direction.
More vibrations = louder sound.

Let's amplify sounds! Turn the page to have a go.

MAKE YOUR OWN 'MEGAPHONE'

Crank up the tunes and make your own home disco with the help of a cardboard tube.

You will need:

- A phone*
- Scissors**
- A kitchen-roll tube or a toilet-roll tube
- Two paper cups
- A pencil

*You might need to borrow one from adult.
**Be careful – ask an adult for help.

Instructions:

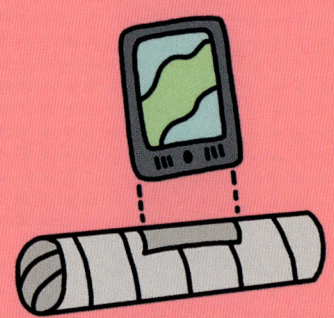

1. On the tube, draw around the end of the phone. Cut out this rectangular slot to fit the phone tightly.

2. Now, on the side of each cup, draw around the end of the tube. Cut out each hole, so the tube can fit tightly into a cup at either end.

34

3. Stand the phone in the slot.

4. Crank up some tunes on the phone and enjoy your 'megaphone'!

Try cutting a small hole into the bottom of the cups. How does this affect the sound quality? And have a go with different sized cups and tubes to see if that changes the sound.

Wei's sister could easily help out and get the party started with a toilet-roll tube and paper cups, or even just by placing the phone inside a glass, to instantly create a 'megaphone'.

35

CALAMITY COMICS

HOW TO MAKE A PHONE CALL WITHOUT A PHONE

8

THE SCIENCE COMIC YOU NEVER KNEW YOU NEEDED — **PHYSICS EDITION**

Tomorrow is Zoe's first day back at school and she can't remember what to do for maths homework! She needs to call her friend to find out, but her dog weed on the phone, and now it doesn't work. Panic! Zoe isn't allowed to go to her friend's house and if she doesn't hand in her homework on time, her teacher is not going to be happy...

Zoe can see into her best friend's bedroom...

...but the roadworks mean she can't hear her.

Drrr! Bang! Clatter!

DO YOU HAVE THE HOMEWORK?!

HUH? YOUR SHOWER'S GONE BERSERK?!

What should Zoe do with all that noise and no phone?

Perhaps you can help? Should Zoe ...

A) TELL THE TEACHER HER DOG ATE HER HOMEWORK?

B) GRAB PAPER CUPS AND SOME STRING?

C) TRY TO DRY HER PHONE IN UNCOOKED RICE?

If you chose A, bad luck. Zoe's teacher has heard this excuse before.
If you chose B, EXCELLENT CHOICE. Zoe can make her own phone.
If you chose C, bad advice — it won't work and could damage Zoe's phone!

WHAT'S THE SCIENCE?

Remember reading about sound travelling as vibrations on page 29? Well, it's also possible to send vibrations over a distance using paper cups and string to get yourself heard without having to strain your voice!

Alexander Graham Bell (1847-1922) invented the telephone back in 1876. You are about to make your very own telephone in the next experiment and guess what? The telephone Alexander Graham Bell invented worked a lot like the one you are going make, only it used electricity to help the sound waves travel from one phone to another.

Ready to make a call?

MAKE YOUR OWN TELEPHONE

Parents won't let you have a phone yet? No worries, two cups and some string will get you there, even if it doesn't have all the apps!

You will need:

- Two paper cups or clean yogurt pots
- Two paperclips
- A pencil*
- A length of string at least three metres long

*Be careful – ask an adult for help when using it to make the hole in the cup.

Sounds can't travel in space as there is no air to pass on the vibrations!

Instructions:

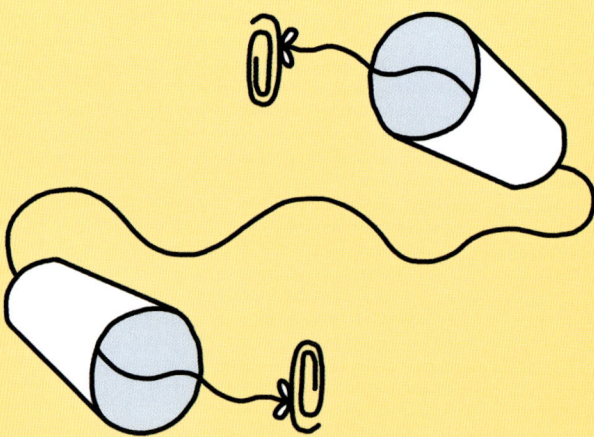

1. Ask an adult to poke a tiny hole in the bottom of each paper cup.

2. Thread the string through the paper cups and tie to a paperclip at each end.

3. Stretch the string so it is tight.

Try the experiment with different materials, such as wool and cotton thread, and bigger cups or pots.

4. Have a chat with your friend on your brand-new phone! Say 'over' when you stop talking to let them know you've finished.

```
If Zoe talks into the cup, the sound vibrations from her voice
   will create vibrations inside the cup. These vibrations are
transferred to the string. They will then travel along the string
  and into the other cup, sending the sound of Zoe's voice to her
       friend's ear at the other end of the string. Clever, eh?
```

CALAMITY COMICS

HOW TO SPY ON SOMEONE

9

THE SCIENCE COMIC YOU NEVER KNEW YOU NEEDED — PHYSICS EDITION

Anika's twin brother has some friends over for a sleepover. It sounds like they are having a great time – she can hear a lot of giggling and rustling. Anika is desperate to know what they are up to . . .

Is Anika's twin brother making something fun? Perhaps a rocket?

Anika needs to find out before he gets them both in trouble.

She creeps down the hallway . . .

But she stops because she doesn't want to wake their mum and get caught out of bed.

Should Anika ...

A) RISK IT AND BURST THROUGH HIS DOOR?

B) GRAB A COUPLE OF MIRRORS?

C) GIVE UP AND GO BACK TO BED?

If you chose A, bad idea – Anika's caught instantly and is now in trouble. If you chose B, BRILLIANT CHOICE. This will help Anika spy on them. If you chose C, Anika escapes trouble but has to wait to discover what her brother and his friends are up to.

WHAT'S THE SCIENCE?

Light is a form of energy. We need it to be able to see. Light travels in a straight line. It **reflects** (bounces off) an object, then enters our eyes so we can see that object. When light is reflected, it changes direction.

Some surfaces are better at reflecting light than others. Smooth, shiny ones are the best. So grabbing two mirrors to create a **periscope** could help Anika. Ready to discover how?

MAKE YOUR OWN PERISCOPE

Once you've finished this experiment, you'll be able to see around corners whenever you want – there will be no sneaking up on you!

You will need:

- Two small mirrors or mirror tiles
- A shoebox
- Scissors*
- A pencil
- Sticky tape

*Be careful – ask an adult for help.

When sailors are on submarines, they use a periscope to see above water when the submarine is still below the water.

Instructions:

1. Remove the shoebox lid and place a mirror on the outside, near the top. Draw around the mirror with the pencil.

2. Place the second mirror at the opposite end, and draw around that (as shown above).

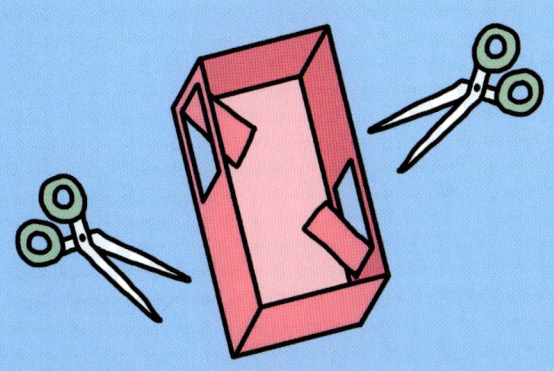

3. Cut out three sides of the drawn sections to make flaps (as above).

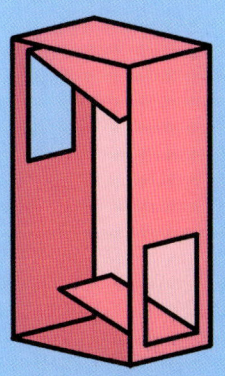

4. Bend the flaps at 45-degree angles.

5. Secure the mirrors onto the slanted flaps with sticky tape.

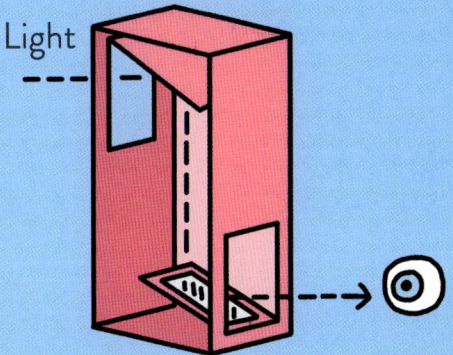

Light

6. Look through the bottom and see if you can see out of the top. If not, adjust the mirrors slightly. Then tape the shoebox lid on and enjoy!

A periscope is clever because it uses the way light bounces off shiny surfaces to help you see, and this is how Anika could see what her brother and his friends are up to! If she doesn't have time, just using a mirror or the back of a spoon to help her peek around the door could work too.**

**Also pretty nifty if you need to watch out for your teacher to get a fart machine out of your classroom before they make it up the corridor (see page 8).

Prrrpt!

43

CALAMITY COMICS

HOW TO TRICK A SHARK

10

THE SCIENCE COMIC YOU NEVER KNEW YOU NEEDED — PHYSICS EDITION

It's time for Rocky and Flynn's swimming lesson, but the lifeguard is panicking because a shark has turned up. That's right! A shark is in the pool and he's set up his towel on a deckchair, put his flip-flops by the stairs and has no intention of moving . . .

The lifeguard is freaking out!

And the pool is starting to look like a yummy bowl of cereal for the shark . . .

How do they trick a shark into leaving the pool?

Especially when the shark looks keen on staying the whole day!

Should the brothers ...

A) POUR A GLASS OF WATER?

B) GET THE SHARK TO CHASE A FRIEND OUT?

C) FIND ANOTHER POOL TO SWIM IN?

If you chose **A**, YOU CHOSE PERFECTLY. They can use the glass to bend light.
If you chose **B**, say goodbye to Rocky and Flynn's friend.
If you chose **C**, this will save Rocky and Flynn, but not everyone else already in the pool.

WHAT'S THE SCIENCE?

Light moves at different speeds through different materials. For example, when light moves from air into water, it slows down. This causes the light to bend, which is called **refraction**, so it enters your eyes from a different angle. Pop a straw into a glass and it will look like the straw is broken! This is also why a pool can appear shallower than it actually is (the light from the bottom of the pool is refracted as it leaves the water).

How does this help Rocky and Flynn? Let's give the science a go and then find out . . .

HAVE A GO AT BENDING LIGHT

Have a go at flipping a drawing of an arrow with a glass of water and the power of refraction. I know this seems like it would never work, but it does!

You will need:

- A piece of paper
- A pen
- Water
- A clear glass tumbler

Light travels faster than anything else in the world – even sound. That's why you can see lightning before you can hear the sound it makes (thunder).

Instructions:

1. Draw an arrow on the piece of paper with your pen.

2. Fill up the glass tumbler with water.

3. Place the glass of water in front of the paper.

4. Look through the glass at the arrow. Has it changed direction?

Make sure the glass is in exactly the right spot, otherwise the arrow will seem the right way around!

Try moving the glass closer to the paper and then further away to see what happens to the arrow.

Reflected light travels from the arrow through the air, then through the glass into the water, and then out of the glass and through the air before it reaches the shark's eyes. So, the light that was at the arrowhead on one side has now flipped to the other side! When the shark decides to go for a ride down the slide, Rocky and Flynn can use a glass of water to flip the arrow to trick him into heading to the exit instead.

CALAMITY COMICS

HOW TO ESCAPE A GORILLA

11

THE SCIENCE COMIC YOU NEVER KNEW YOU NEEDED — PHYSICS EDITION

Mo and his family are on the way home from a weekend away when they take a wrong turn and are faced with an angry gorilla. They've only gone straight into a jungle! Mo's dad is freaking out because the sat nav keeps telling them to turn around, but there's another angry gorilla approaching from behind!

Mo can see a bridge that will take his family straight out of the jungle . . .

But Mo's mum reckons their car is too heavy to make it across because his dad packed too much stuff!

There's also a bridge over ostrich eggshells. His dad isn't keen on that one either . . .

. . . but the gorillas are looking more menacing by the second.

What's the best decision? Should they ...

A) GO OVER THE RICKETY BRIDGE?

B) GO OVER THE EGGSHELL BRIDGE?

C) GET OUT OF THE CAR AND ASK FOR DIRECTIONS?

If you chose A, bad idea. Mo's dad's weighty packing means the minute the car hits the middle of the bridge, they will all tumble down into the ravine. If you chose B, WELL DONE! The giant ostrich eggs help to make the bridge strong. If you chose C, sadly the gorillas chase Mo into the jungle.

WHAT'S THE SCIENCE?

You may have noticed that bridges often look like arches. That's because the shape of an arch helps spread the weight of a vehicle, or anything really, that's on top, by allowing the sides to help support the structure. The ancient Romans loved using arches as bridges, over 2,000 years ago, too.

Now what's this got to do with eggshells? Well, if you look closely at an egg, you will notice it has an arch shape at either end. The egg is nature's arch. And believe it or not, you are about to discover just how strong an eggshell can be . . .

HOW STRONG IS AN EGGSHELL BRIDGE?

Find out the super strength of the eggshell in this 'egg-cellent' experiment.

You will need:

- A bowl
- A pile of books or magazines
- Scissors*
- Four eggs (uncooked)

*Be careful – ask an adult for help.

Instructions:

1. Carefully crack the eggs into a bowl, trying to keep the shell in two half pieces. Save the yolk and whites in case you fancy baking a cake later.

2. Wash the eggshells carefully and leave them to dry.

3. Ask an adult to help you trim the eggshells' edges so they are neat.

4. Place the eggshells on a table in a square, so that each eggshell half is a corner of the square.

5. Gently place a book on top of the eggshells, making sure they are centred under the book.

6. Place another book on top of that book.

7. Then another... Then another... Keep going until you break the eggshells. How many books did it take?

The eggshell bridge is the best choice because having the arches supporting the beam of wood means it could take more weight and hold up a longer beam of wood without bending in the middle. As long as the ostrich eggs are level with the ground, it's likely that the eggs would support the bridge rather than get crushed. Phew!

CALAMITY COMICS

HOW TO SCARE OFF AN ALIEN INVASION

THE SCIENCE COMIC YOU NEVER KNEW YOU NEEDED — **PHYSICS EDITION**

Ava's family are all looking forward to a movie night. The popcorn is buttered and the hot chocolates are steaming. But just as they put on the telly, a news alert flashes up on the screen: ALIENS ARE ON THE WAY!

Ava is not going to let visitors from outer space ruin movie night . . .

Especially as the last one was ruined by Ava's granny continually farting.

Should Ava ...

A) JUST WATCH THE MOVIE?

B) MAKE SHADOW PUPPETS?

C) HIDE?

If you chose A, this starts off well but just at the crucial moment in the movie, the aliens arrive . . .

If you chose B, WELL DONE! Woo hoo - Ava can scare those aliens away!

If you chose C, this works until Granny's farts give everyone away and the aliens move in and Ava's family never get to watch what they want.

WHAT'S THE SCIENCE?

Light can only pass through some materials. **Transparent** materials, like glass, let light shine through. **Translucent** materials allow light through, but you can't see through them as they scatter some of the light. And **opaque** materials, like wood or thick paper, block light completely. Grab a torch and different objects to test this out.

Shadows are dark shapes that appear on a surface when an opaque object blocks light. Shadows change depending on the direction of the light and how near or far the light is from the object. The smaller the object's distance from the light, the bigger the shadow (because the object blocks more light from the lamp).

Ready to see how some super shadows could help Ava?

CREATE YOUR OWN SHADOW PUPPETS

Get ready to fight off an alien invasion with some super-creative shadow shapes – all made yourself!

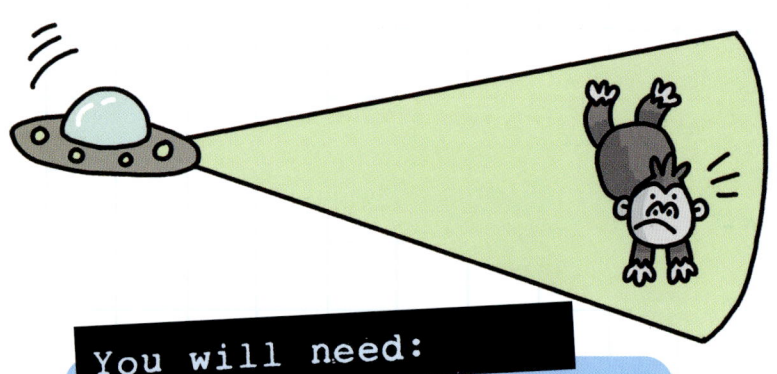

Three and half thousand years ago, the ancient Egyptians used shadows to tell the time, using a device called a sundial. Make your own by popping a pencil through the middle of a paper plate. Then, outside on a sunny day, mark where the shadow falls on each hour.

You will need:

- A wall
- A desk lamp or torch
- A table

Ye olde sundial watch

Instructions:

1. Ask an adult to help you place the table by a wall. Then put the torch or lamp on the table so the light shines on the wall.

2. Dim all the other lights. Don't look directly at the light.

3. Use your hands or body to make shapes in front of the light and have fun seeing the shadows form.

By stringing up a huge sheet with a torch shining on it, Ava's family can create creepy black silhouettes with paper or their bodies to scare off the aliens. The closer the light is to the paper or person, the more giant the shadow looks!

CALAMITY COMICS

HOW TO SAVE YOUR GRANNY FROM A RUNAWAY TRAIN

13

THE SCIENCE COMIC YOU NEVER KNEW YOU NEEDED — **PHYSICS EDITION**

Oh no! Amy's granny was on her way out for an afternoon of football. (She wanted to practise her shots at goal as she had just been selected to play for the over 95s at her local football club.) But her car broke down on a railway crossing. Now she's underneath the bonnet trying to fix it, but Amy's just heard news that a runaway train is heading straight for Granny!

Granny has her headphones on and the music is **TOO LOUD** . . .

And she has no idea the runaway train is heading straight for her.

She can't hear everyone yelling at her to get to safety . . .

Can you help? Should Amy ...

A) SEND A SUPERCHARGED TRAIN DOWN THE TRACK?

B) PANIC?

C) ADVERTISE FOR ANOTHER GRANNY?

If you chose A, YOU DID IT! An electromagnet will save Granny!
If you chose B, uh-oh, panicking NEVER WORKS!
If you chose C, how could you?! There will only ever be one Granny!

WHAT'S THE SCIENCE?

Boost a train with a magnet! Trains are pretty fast and pretty heavy, though, so the magnet holding up your artwork on the fridge is not going to be too helpful - we need an **electromagnet**.

A homemade electromagnet can hold a paperclip (1g), but it's possible to make a super strong one. For example, an electromagnet at a scrapyard can hold a car (around 1,000kg)!

Let's put the science to work with an experiment.

MAKE YOUR OWN ELECTROMAGNET

You won't be able to stop a speeding train with this experiment, but you will be able to turn a nail into a magnet, which is fun.

You will need:

- Thinly insulated copper wire (about 1m)*
- An AA 1.5v battery*
- A 7.5cm steel nail*
- A metal paperclip
- Sticky tape
- Scissors or wire strippers*

*Be careful - ask an adult for help.

We can thank British scientist Michael Faraday (1791–1867) for discovering how to create an electromagnet. He also invented the rubber party balloon!

Instructions:

1. Tap the nail against a paperclip. It won't attract the paperclip because the nail is not magnetic.

2. Wrap the wire tightly around the nail, leaving about 15cm of wire free at either end.

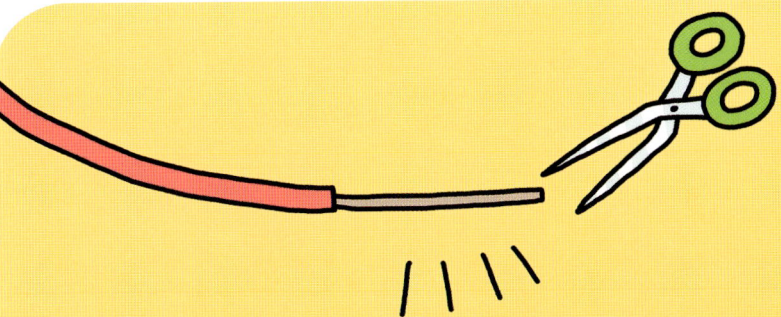

3. Ask an adult to use scissors to score the coating of each end of the wire and then drag off the plastic layer. An adult could also use wire strippers to do this.

4. Tape the bare metal ends of the wire to each end of the battery.

5. Your nail should now be an electromagnet and pick up the paperclip!

Turn the electromagnet on and off by disconnecting and reconnecting the wire from the battery.

If Amy tightly wound a really, really, really long wire around a super-speedy steel train and attached it to a ginormous battery with a huge electric current, she would turn the train into a huge electromagnet. Okay, so this wouldn't be very practical or safe, but in theory, if the electromagnetic train was sent down the tracks after the steel runaway train, it could slow it down and pull it back using magnetic attraction. And save Amy's granny from becoming as squished as a squashed banana!

GLOSSARY

AIR RESISTANCE: The force of the air pushing against a moving object.

AMPLIFY: To make something louder.

ATTRACT: To pull together.

COMPASS: A tool to help you find the right direction.

EFFORT: The force needed to move something.

ELECTROMAGNET: A type of magnet where the magnetic field is created by electricity.

FRICTION: The force that works against a moving object.

FULCRUM: The point on which a lever balances, moves or turns.

GRAVITY: A pulling force that works on all objects and keeps our feet on the ground.

LEVER: A long object that rests on a fulcrum.

MAGNET: A rock or metal that attracts other metals or rocks towards it.

OPAQUE: Does not allow light through, like brick.

PERISCOPE: An object that helps you see around corners and over walls using the laws of reflection.

PULLEY: A mechanism that changes the direction of the force required to lift an object.

REFLECT: Light bouncing off an object.

REFRACTION: Light changing direction as it moves from one material to another.

REPEL: To push apart.

SHADOWS: Dark shapes that appear on a surface when an opaque object blocks light.

SOUND WAVES: Vibrations of air molecules that cause us to hear a sound when they reach our ears.

TRANSLUCENT: Scatters light as it passes through the material, like frosted glass or frosted plastic.

TRANSPARENT: Lets light shine right through it, like glass.

INDEX

A
air resistance 9, 10-11, 60
arch 49, 51

B
Bassi, Laura 6
Bell, Alexander Graham 37
bridge 49, 50-51

C
compass 21, 22-23, 60

E
Earth 21, 22
effort 13, 15, 60
Egyptians, ancient 17, 54
electricity 29, 37, 59, 60
electromagnet 57, 58-59, 60
energy 41, 60

F
Faraday, Michael 58
forces 9, 13, 17, 25, 60
friction 25, 26-27, 60
fulcrum 13, 14-15, 60

G
gravity 9, 60

L
lever 13, 14-15, 60
light 41, 43, 45, 46-47, 53, 54-55, 60

M
magnet 21, 22, 57, 58-59, 60
megaphone 33, 34-35
metal 21, 22, 23, 58, 59, 60
mirror 41, 42-43

N
Newton, Isaac 25
north (and south) 22-23

P
parachute 9, 10-11
periscope 41, 42-43, 60
pulley 17, 18-19, 60

R
reflection 41, 60
refraction 45, 46-47, 60
Romans, ancient 49

S
seesaw 13, 14-15
shadow 53, 54-55, 60
sound 29, 30-31, 33, 35, 37, 38-39, 46, 60
space 9, 38
submarine 42
sundial 54

T
telephone 37, 38-39

V
vibration 29, 30, 33, 37, 38-39